Thanks to God and my family who always stood by me!

Contents

36 SECRETS HR DEPARTMENT NEVER TELLS YOU!

INTRODUCTION:

It gives me great pleasure to write my third book! A lot of friends and close relatives have been asking me pen down a good book on Human Resources. With over 20 years of experience in HR, believe me, I've seen it all!

Employees often look upon Human Resources Department as a go-to place, to solve issues or just simply to complaint about a particular issue!

Love HR or hate HR...but you can't ignore HR!

So, below I list SECRETS (If you can call that), to better understand the HR department and especially be prepared the next time you speak to your HR Manager!

This book will be useful for anyone planning to attend interviews or even to employees who work in companies. By understanding how HR works, you increase your chance to get selected!
And by knowing what HR expects of you in a company, you can play your cards right for that next promotion!

1

Secret 1:

DON'T STAY UNEMPLOYED FOR TOO LONG!

If at all you are unemployed for over 6 months while applying for a job, make sure you have a valid explanation. If its maternity leaves, that's an exception! But anything otherwise, like giving reasons that you wanted a break etc. will definitely go against you.

HR looks for consistency in resumes. And changing too many jobs is a big NO too.

"If you think hiring professionals is expensive, try hiring amateurs."
– Anonymous

Secret 2

HR MANAGERS ARE BIASED

Does it mean that HR Managers will pick candidates they like? It a YES and NO actually. HR Managers will prefer candidates who have connections in the same office as it gives more reliability to the hiring process. And most importantly, if the newly hired employee vanishes after a month, then we know whom to catch!!!

*"Human Resources isn't a thing we do. It's the thing that runs our business." – **Steve Wynn**, Wynn Las Vegas*

Secret 3

OH YES, AGE DOES MATTER!

Unless it's a senior profile, HR will prefer to hire a younger person for Junior and Mid-senior levels. The reason being that younger talents are more keep to learn and put in more working hours. Solution: Avoid mentioning your age on your resume and DO NOT give details about your graduation year. If asked, mention it in the face-to-face interview. It's not that you can't get that job, however you do need to play your card right!

*"Time spent on hiring, is time well spent." – **Robert Half***

Secret 4

DON'T MENTION FAMILY TIES.

I remember interviewing a candidate quite recently whose profile was excellent. The only reason I rejected him was because 80% of the time, all he spoke about was his family – his kids, his dog and what his hobbies were. HR loves to hear about your family but to a limit. We never really want too many personal details. Rather, speak about how you can contribute towards the company. Period. That's why you are here in the first place!

> *"The hardest challenge being an HR is that sometimes you have to be the LAWYER, the JUDGE and the HANGMAN." –* ***Hassan Choughari***

Secret 5

JAMES BOND!

Well, you dont have to dress up as James Bond to get the job, but personal grooming and appearances count! HR observes EVERYTHING! And I mean everything like your shoes? Are they polished?

The shirt you are wearing? Is it ironed well?

Is the perfume too strong?

If you are a smoker, kindly take care of your breath!

Are you well shaved? Or is your beard trimmed?

For a Sales position, I had to reject quite a few candidates because he wanted in wearing casual wear. If they cannot take time to come well dressed, where is their commitment or interest?

Be your best and ace that interview!

> "Without the right succession planning put to play in human resources, we build for the future without a future." – **Mmanti Umoh**

Secret 6

BLAME GAME!

When asked as to why you left your previous Job, never blame anyone especially your old boss! HR judges you on how you accept challenges in life. The last thing HR wants is a person who always complaints. Does not reflect well.

Solution: Be frank but speak about the positives you got from your previous job! HR will appreciate that.

"Children imitate their parents, employees their managers." – ***Amit Kalantri***

Secret 7

NEVER BE YOURSELF!!!

Normally, they say to be yourself, never put on a false self etc. But my advice is stick to your strongest points, stress that during interviews and talk about what you can contribute. When asked about your weakness, just tell them how that weakness ADDS as a strength to your decision making process.

Example: Say your weakness if that you are a workaholic which in turn makes you NOT balance family life. Incases (like mine!) it's true! But see any weakness which BENEFITS the company. If you really say that you have a weakness as in smoking or addicted to mobiles, then it's an issue!

Coat your answer to what HR wants to hear. But be truthful.

Never say I don't have a weakness! HR will see you through you and a person who is matured, will know his/her weakness. That is why he has reached the position he/she is in. No one is perfect and HR knows that!

"The body may be bought with a paycheck but the heart is earned with a purpose." – **Angela Lynne Craig**

Secret 8

SOCIAL MEDIA POSTS – WILL SURELY HURT YOU!

Be very careful what you post in Social Media sites. In most cases HR checks on your social media sites BEFORE they call you for an Interview. If there are any comments on racism or political overtones, them HR will prefer to turn you down.

Solution: Delete all such posts one week before the interview. Better still, before applying!

*"If you pay peanuts, you get monkeys."— **Chinese Proverb***

Secret 9

YOU ARE WATCHED ALWAYS

During your tenure in any company, employees feel that they can get away with small issues, and stay relaxed. Believe me, as long as you are within the company premises, HR does not need a physical camera to keep a watch on you! HR or top management have their ways to see what you do on your computer or your behavior with that difficult colleague ALWAYS! Sometimes, you are informed; otherwise, HR waits to inform you at the right time. So, be professional at all times.

"Believe in yourself and all that you are. Know that there is something inside you that is greater than any obstacle." — Christian D. Larson

Secret 10

HANDSHAKE MATTERS!

This is true especially during Interviews. A firm handshake tells HR that you are reliable and can get the Job done.

Be very attentive to this detail. A loose hand shake shows lack of interest and commitment.

Make your handshake count even if you feel you will not get that job. HR will appreciate that!

"Alone we can do so little, together we can do so much." — Helen Keller

Secret 11

BODY LANGUAGE COUNTS TOO!

This is applicable not only at the time of interviews, but also when employed.

Do you cross your hands and sit while talking? (Shows that you are not open)

Do you smile showing your tooth – a full smile or just a small smile? (Shows your commitment)

Do you lean forward and talk? (Shows too much eagerness)

Do you maintain eye contact? (Shows boldness) – I prefer it if you DO NOT stare but rather look at the eyes, got it?

Read some good books on Body Language. It will really help you in getting your positive vibes across.

"The quality of a leader is reflected in the standards they set for themselves." — Ray Kroc

12

Secret 12

HANDWRITING ANALYSIS

Do you know why HR normally insists that you fill out that Personal details form, especially when you have already submitted your resume? The truth is most experienced HR professionals know Handwriting Analysis. They can read your personality and can know if you are a fit for a particular job. Example: If it's a marketing candidate they look for, if your writing shows that you are an introvert, then, they might not select you.

"Good management is the art of making problems so interesting and their solutions so constructive that everyone wants to get to work and deal with them." — Paul Hawkin

Secret 13

YOUR WEIGHT MATTERS TOO!

This is especially true in roles where you have to interact with customers over the counter or as Tour Managers. HR worries as to, what the customer will think and in most cases, if you are the ambassadors of the company (Unless its wrestling!)
Then, there is little hope that you might get that dream job!

> "You cannot push anyone up the ladder unless he is willing to climb." — Andrew Carnegie

Secret 14

COMPANIES, NOT NGOs !

During my career I had come across many candidates explaining as to why they need that particular job, and their financial difficulties they are facing. HR does care but the bottom line is, HR will tend to ignore such candidates because the company does not work on charity. Its not a personal decision.

If you have the skill and experience with a right attitude, that's all that maters!

"True motivation comes from achievement, personal development, job satisfaction, and recognition." — Frederick Herzberg

Secret 15

AVOID INTER OFFICE RELATIONSHIPS

HR does not like interoffice relationships for the simple reason that it shifts the focus from work and makes you miss deadlines! HR might not take an official action but this will be discussed at the time of your Performance Review!

If you do find lady love or Mr. Romeo at your office place, try your nest to keep it professional! (Unless you plan to quit)

"The conventional definition of management is getting work done through people, but real management is developing people through work." — Agha Hasan Abedi

Secret 16

NEVER DISCUSS ISSUES IN THE RESTROOM!

Especially true for ladies! Word gets around and the last thing you want to be known as the 'Queen of Gossip'! So, keep talks minimum and stay in the good books of the Management!

"Hire people who are better than you are, then leave them to get on with it. Look for people who will aim for the remarkable, who will not settle for the routine." — David Ogilvy

Secret 17

THERE ARE 2 PARALLEL HIRING PROCESS

Yes, you heard that right! No matter how many candidates apply for a position, internal references DO COUNT!

It's no surprise that HR spends their annual budget for Referral Programs and if you are applying for that job, quickly make friends with any employee working in that particular company. Your chances of getting hired increases without any doubt!

"Innovation distinguishes between a leader and a follower." — Steve Jobs

Secret 18

EMERGENCY LEAVES

HR always sees an employee who often takes EL as an employee, who lacks discipline!
Make sure you do not over use the EL facility given in the company.
Some employees do misuse this benefit and HR knows this for a fact.

"If everyone is moving forward together, then success takes care of itself." — Henry Ford

---

Secret 19

RESUME KEYWORDS

Always remember, when you create your resume, make KEYWORDS, put in in BOLD and make sure it stands out. HR departments gets hundreds or resumes a day, and when the HR goes through the resume, he looks only for Key words. HR does not have time to read the entire resume in detail,

You could highlight your experience achievements, your strengths and ALWAYS include a cover letter as to why you fit the job. As per statistics 53.5% of the resumes are rejected if there is no cover letter attached.

So, make yourself count!

"Individual commitment to a group effort–that is what makes a team work, a company work, a society work, a civilization work." — Vince Lombardi

Secret 20

NEVER OFFER BENEFITS FOR HR

This simply means that never offer the HR manager gifts or bribe to get the job. Even if you do succeed to get the Job, the HR manager will soon be fired and your employment selection will be in review. Let your talent speak for itself. Generally HR likes people with ethics and that should reflect in your actions.

"Unless you try to do something beyond what you have already mastered, you will never grow." — Ralph Waldo Emerson

Secret 21:

APPLICATIONS SUBMITTED

HR always know if you have submitted more than 1 application for a position. Maybe you have submitted for multiple positions. My advise: Never apply for many position. Apply for the one position you have a better chance of getting.

Applying for many positions shows that you are desperate for work, and HR will surely overlook your application.

"Leadership is not about a title or a designation. It's about impact, influence and inspiration. Impact involves getting results, influence is about spreading the passion you have for your work, and you have to inspire team-mates and customers." — Robin S. Sharma

Secret 22

REFERENCE CHECK DO HAPPEN

If you thought that reference checks do not happen often, think again! Reference checks are done by HR by an external agency or directly. And HR even does the reference checks for existing employees on random basis.

Always better not to fake your experience /educational certificates and be straight. Better not to get that job than to be terminated!!

"Human Resources isn't a thing we do. It's the thing that runs our business."

- Steve Wynn, CEO of Wynn Resorts Limited

Secret 23:

REWARDS AND RECOGNITATION

Though your Reporting Manager suggests your name for the R & R program, HR always has a say!

Attendance, late coming etc plays a vital role in deciding that recognition for you.

Always keep HR informed for unscheduled leaves and make sure HR is informed if you face any difficulties at work. HR will help and even if you do have an issue with your Reporting Manager, HR can help.

Always approach HR for any issue and you will be in the good books of HR!

"Recruitment IS marketing. If you're a recruiter nowadays and you don't see yourself as a marketer, you're in the wrong profession."

- Matthew Jeffrey, Global head of sourcing and employment brand at SAP

Secret 24:

HR RECRUITS NUT DEPARTMENTAL HEADS MAKE THE FINAL CALL

HR can shortlist a prospective candidate but always remembers that the final decision will rest with the Reporting Manager or Management.
If the candidate is not technically sound or has an attitude, no matter how talented otherwise, he will be rejected. So, take every stage of Interview seriously!

"Leadership and learning are indispensable to each other." — John Fitzgerald Kennedy

Secret 25

DON'T GET TOO FRIENDLY

HR always like to keep a professional relationship. Getting too friendly with HR is not advisable. Any informal discussion outside office is ok, but limit your conversations to a professional level in office. If HR wants to know about your wellbeing, you can always speak and share.
HR does care for its employees and shows empathy. But in most cases they are not there to solve your personal problems! But they are good listeners!

"Nothing we do is more important than hiring and developing people. At the end of the day, you bet on people, not on strategies."

- Lawrence Bossidy, Former COO of General Electric

Secret 26

NEVER BORROW MONEY FROM YOUR COLLEGUES

HR hates people who borrow money and in most cases, fail to return the same. NEVER as HR for a personal loan, it's the worst thing you can do!
In case you do require urgent money, every company has emergency finds and you can ask HR to help you get that. HR will help in most cases.

"The competition to hire the best will increase in the years ahead. Companies that give extra flexibility to their employees will have the edge in this area."

- Bill Gates, Founder of Microsoft Corporation

Secret 27

OFFICE BLUES!

Before you shoot out that mail telling that HR can implement all policies but fail to keep the restroom clean or any other repair issues, speak to HR directly. HR appreciates employees who directly approach and speak about the issue, rather that sending a mail to everyone in the office.

Sending official mail is important but try to speak to HR first. HR will look into the issue personally.

Sending mail is the second step. HR likes to hear you out first!

"You Learn More From Failure Than From Success. Don't Let It Stop You. Failure Builds Character." – Unknown

Secret 28

BE PROFESSIONAL

Be professional at all time. HR will not just evaluate you on your Performance Appraisals.

HR will see on a daily basis if you are wearing your ID card, your appearance and how you relate to your colleagues.

Be positive and if you are an employee, think like a manager and don't be afraid to take responsibility.

HR loves employees who think about the company first.

"Train people well enough so they can leave, treat them well enough so they don't want to."

- Richard Branson, Founder of Virgin Group

Secret 29:

RESIGNATION

In case you decide to move on, discuss with HR personally BEFORE you hand over that resignation.

HR appreciates employees who are frank and exit interviews happen normally before an employee gives in the paper.

HR will, in most cases, clear any misunderstandings but in case you have decided to move on HR will help you finish your exit formalities at the earliest.

Remember even if you do quit and join a new company, HR will still be involved to give that referral check status report.

So, be frank and HR will appreciate that.

"If you hire good people, give them good jobs, and pay them good wages, generally something good is going to happen."

- James Sinegal, Co-founder and former CEO of Costco Wholesale Corporation

Secret 30

HR IS PART OF THE MANAGEMENT

Employees always expect HR to support the employees and speak for them to the Management.

The fact is HR is part of the Management. HR is the spokes person and feedback mechanism for the Top Management. All polices and welfare benefits are aligned with the Managements approval.

Top Management rarely has time to meet each employee and discuss issues. That's where HR comes in.

HR will definitely look into your issues but if it is not in alignment with the Company's goal and strategy, it's really helpless to force HR to speak to Management.

So remember, our feedbacks count but HR will discuss with Top Management and both will make the final decision.

> "The secret of my success is that we have gone to exceptional lengths to hire the best people in the world."
>
> - Steve Jobs, Chairman, CEO and co-founder of Apple

Secret 31

DISCIPLINE

HR always appreciates employees who accept disciplinary actions gracefully. It not only shows that you have character but also shows that you can handle stress.

So the next time you get a warning letter from HR, kindly restrain from arguing and make sure the mistake is repeated.

If it's a misunderstanding, HR will realize it and in most cases help to resolve in time. Be patient and trust HR.

HR loves employees with character. But hate people who crib!

"Acquiring the right talent is the most important key to growth. Hiring was - and still is - the most important thing we do."

- Marc Bennioff, Founder, Chairman and co-CEO of Salesforce

Secret 33

HR LOVES TO SEE YOU GROW

Many employees feel that HR never cares for the employees grow, or HR implements too many policies!

Truth is HR wants each employee to learn, grow and be positive. That will reflect in the company's growth and further the employee's career prospects.

HR loves to give you promotions and salary hikes. But most employees are greedy and try to get it before the right time. Be patient.

HR will always be there for you!

"Recently, I was asked if I was going to fire an employee who made a mistake that cost the company $600,000. No, I replied, I just spent $600,000 training him. Why would I want somebody to hire his experience?"

- Thomas John Watson Sr., Former chairman and CEO of IBM

Secret: 34

HR Managers are humans too!

Have no doubt, no matter how cold a HR manager may sound or makes those policies you crib about, they actually know your pain! Remember, they are just doing a professional job, and in their hearts, they CARE.

They might even have a drink with you after office hours, and meet your family or buy a bone for your dog! But never discuss office work during your evenings if you decide to spend time together.

Health is the greatest gift, contentment the greatest wealth, faithfulness the best relationship - Buddha

Secret 35:

OFFICE POLITICS

If at all you hear any gossip, NEVER, and I mean NEVER tell it to HR.

HR normally has got the information beforehand and even if not, HR hates employees who spread news!

If its some information which affects the company as a whole, you could share it – Provided its from a reliable source!

Nothing is impossible, the word itself says 'I'm possible'! By Audrey Hepburn

Secret 36

HR PROFESSIONALS ARE NOT THE HIGHEST PAID PROFESSIONALS!

Fact is HR professionals worldwide are paid good, but it all depends on experience, benefits etc.

I know an experienced HR professional working for a small salary but his benefits far exceeds his income! It all depends on the HR professional's priorities in life and what gives him Job satisfaction!

With self-discipline most anything is possible - Theodore Roosevelt

BONUS CHAPTER!!!

10 WAYS TO ACE THAT INTERVIEW!!

1.   APPLY FOR THE JOB YOU ARE PASSIONATE ABOUT

In most cases, candidates apply for the job because of financial commitments and earn. They miss a very import point – Always apply for a Job you are passionate about and you never have to work a single day in your life!!
Even if you are a fresher or without experience, show the HR manager that you are willing to learn and thrown in those extra hours. You will be selected!

2   CREATE AN ACE RESUME!

Your resume is the key that opens the door for an interview. Make sure there are no grammar mistakes and include a cover letter.
Nothing is more important than submitting a professional resume.

3.   PREPARE -PREPARE-PREPARE

Before you attend that all-important interview, preparation is 70% of the work done. Genuinely study the companies Objectives, goals and see where the company can improve in the next 2 years. Make a study and the more knowledge you have about the company, the more confident you will be at the interview.

4.   DRESS CODE

At the time of Interview make sure you ask before hand the dress code. This can be done by calling the HR dept. or the receptionist. Ask in friendly terms the dress code, normally, they will tell you!

5.   SEND A THANK YOU NOTE

After the interview, send a small thank you note to the person who had interviewed you! It does not matter even if you do not get the job or if the interview went satisfactory. This good gesture will always be remembered! And you will be considered for future positions.

6.   BE POSITIVE

At times, we apply and wait to be called for an interview. And the call never comes. Even if we are shortlisted, we sometimes don't get selected.
Positive thoughts bring positive results. Be patient. And you will get the right job.

7.   NETWORK

Make connections. Contacts friends, ex-colleagues and ask for referrals. Small gestures bring BIG results. Don't fight this battle alone. Take support. Use the right contacts to land your dream job!

8.   THINK SPIRITUAL

Believe in yourself Believe that a Higher Power is guiding you. Mediate. Listen to good music. Read good books to relax. All this increases your positive energy and will draw that dream job to you soon!

9   ATTITUDE IS EVERYTHING

Have a positive learning attitude. Have an attitude to share and be involved in social services. Your social activities will surely be noticed via your social media pages (twitter/Facebook etc.) and will be an asset when you apply for your dream job.

10.   APPLY ON THE COMPANY WEBSITES DIRECTLY

Wherever possible apply directly in Company websites on their career section. Response is quicker and HR will know that you have visited their website too.

CONCLUSION

Congratulations! You have finally finished this book and now know how an HR professional thinks and what they expect of you!

Even if you remember 70% of the points given in this book, it will take you a long way in realizing you to get that dream job!

Even as an employee, you are greatly benefit with the secrets given above.

Not all HR Mangers will speak openly about the points I noted above. Some may argue! But the points are based on my 20 years of HR experience working for various companies.

Arun Mathews is a HR professional and works for a Educational Travel Company called Crazy Holidays in Bangalore (India). He stays with his wife and two daughters. He has done his MBA (HR) and is gifted in putting complex terms into simple language.

If you loved reading this book, kindly leave a honest feedback on Amazon or online for me! This will help the book reach out to more people and help them.

You can contact me for any advice/feedbacks on
arunmathewshr@gmail.com

Take Care,
Arun Mathews

Printed in Great Britain
by Amazon